Senses

KINGFISHER

a Houghton Mifflin Company imprint
222 Berkeley Street
Boston, Massachusetts 02116
www.houghtonmifflinbooks.com

First published in 2004
2 4 6 8 10 9 7 5 3 1

1TR/0504/PROSP/RNB(RNB)/140MA/F

LIBRARY OF CONGRESS CATALOGING-IN-PUBLICATION DATA
has been applied for.

ISBN 0-7534-5771-7

Editor: Catherine Brereton
Coordinating editor: Caitlin Doyle
Senior designer: Peter Clayman
Cover designer: Poppy Jenkins
Picture researcher: Rachael Swann
Illustrations: Sebastien Quigley (Linden Artists)
DTP coordinator: Sarah Pfitzner
DTP operator: Primrose Burton
Artwork archivists: Wendy Allison, Jenny Lord
Senior production controller: Oonagh Phelan
Indexer and proofreader: Sheila Clewley

Printed in China

Acknowledgments
The Publisher would like to thank the following for permission to reproduce their material.
Every care has been taken to trace copyright holders. However, if there have been unintentional omissions or failure
to trace copyright holders, we apologize and will, if informed, endeavor to make corrections in any future edition.
b = bottom, *c* = center, *l* = left, *t* = top, *r* = right

Photographs: 1 Corbis; 2–3 Michael K. Nichols/National Geographic; 4–5 Raymond Gehman/National Geographic; 6–7 Alamy Images;
9*r* Digital Vision; 10*cl* Adam Hart-Davis/Science Photo Library; 10–11*b* Sean Murphy/Getty Images; 12*l* Piers Cavendish/ardea.com;
12–13*t* DiMaggio/Kalish/Corbis; 13*br* Jeff Lepore/Science Photo Library; 14*bl* NHPA/James Carmichael Jr; 14–15*tc* NHPA/Stephen Dalton;
15*br* NHPA/Nigel J. Dennis; 17*br* Susumu Nishinaga/Science Photo Library; 18*l* Mark Baker/Reuters; 18–19*b* Roy Morsch/Corbis; 19*tr* Tony
Marshall/EMPICS Sports Photo Agency; 20*l* NHPA/William Paton; 20–21*c* NHPA/Daryl Balfour; 21*br* Duncan McEwan/Nature Picture Library;
22*bl(l)* Joel W. Rogers/Corbis; 22*bl(r)* Nick Gordon/ardea.com; 22–23*t* NHPA/ANT Photo Library; 23*br* Georgettte Douwma/Getty Images;
24*bl* NHPA/Stephen Dalton; 25*tr* NHPA/ANT Photo Library; 25*br* Dietmar Nill/Nature Picture Library; 26*l* Craig Hammel/Corbis;
27*t* BSIP VEM/Science Photo Library; 27*br* Suzanne & Nick Geary/Getty Images; 28*tl* François Gohier/ardea.com; 28–29*b* NHPA/Guy
Edwardes; 29*tr* NHPA/Ann & Steve Toon; 30–31*b* Pascal Goetgheluck/ardea.com; 31*tr* John Downer Productions/Nature Picture Library;
31*br* Roy Morsch/Corbis; 32*br* Corbis; 33*b* Omikron/Science Photo Library; 34*l* NHPA/Martin Harvey; 34–35*b* NHPA/T. Kitchin & V. Hurst;
35*tr* Matthew Oldfield, Scubazoo/Science Photo Library; 37*tl* Phil Jude/Science Photo Library; 38*l* Angelo Cavalli/Getty Images
and Ryan Mcvay/Getty Images; 38–39*b* NHPA/Kevin Schafer; 39*tr* Dr. Jeremy Burgess/Science Photo Library;
48 Ralph A. Clevenger/Corbis.

Cover photography by Daniel Pangbourne.
Commissioned photography on pages 33, 36 and 42–47 by Andy Crawford.
Project maker and photo shoot coordinator: Miranda Kennedy.
Thank you to models Corey Addai, Anastasia Mitchell,
Sonnie Nash, and Shannon Porter.

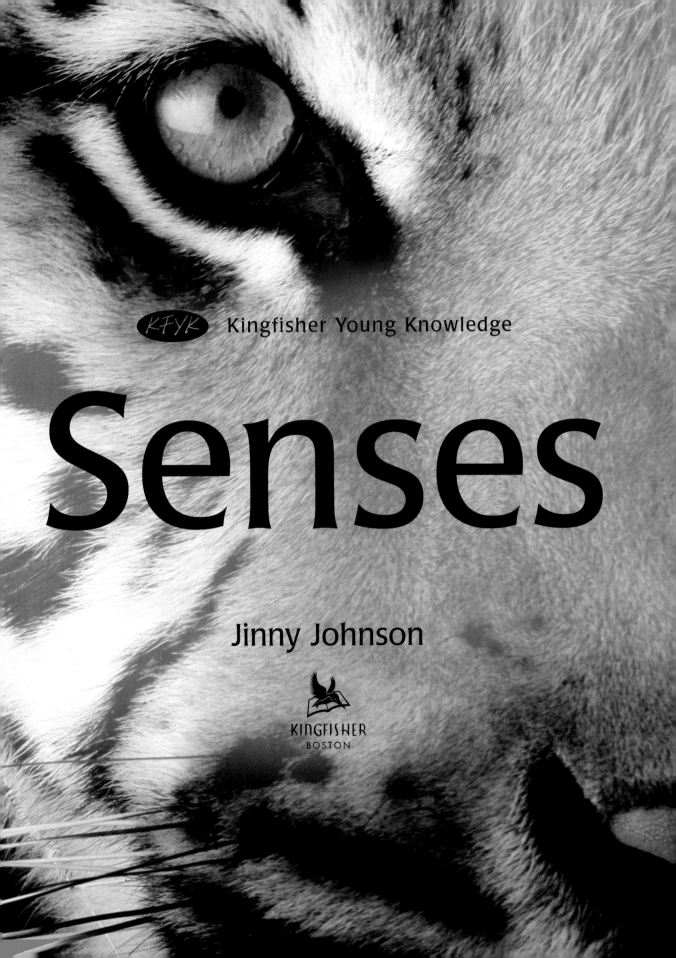

Kingfisher Young Knowledge

Senses

Jinny Johnson

KINGFISHER
BOSTON

Contents

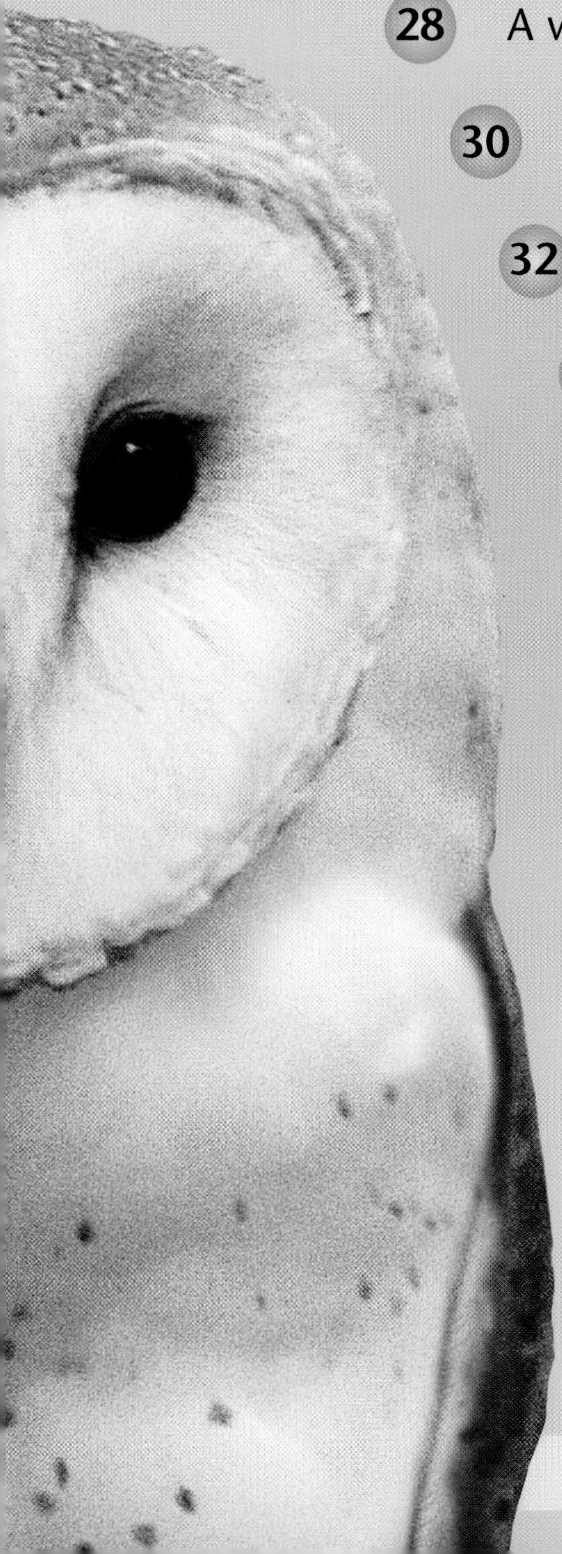

What are senses?

Imagine what the world would be like if you could not see things or hear your friends talking or if you could not smell and taste your food. We do not usually think about our senses, but they tell us what is going on around us. We have five main senses. They are sight, hearing, smell, taste, and touch.

Super senses

Animals have senses too. Some animals have even better senses than we do. Dogs can hear sounds that humans cannot, and they have a much stronger sense of smell.

Using senses

This boy can see his dog's big brown eyes, feel his soft fur, and hear his whimpering sounds. He can also smell the roses in the background and can probably smell his dog.

The sense center

Your brain controls your senses. Messages travel from your eyes, ears, nose, tongue, and skin to tell your brain what is going on. These messages travel along special pathways in the body called nerves.

brain

nerves

Messages to the brain

Nerves go from the brain to all parts of your body. A message can zoom along the nerves to the brain in a tiny fraction of a second.

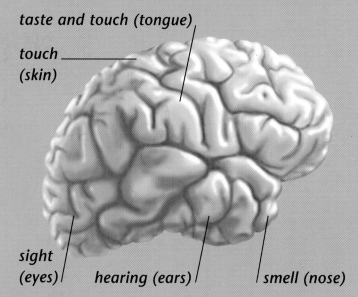

taste and touch (tongue)

*touch _____
(skin)*

*sight
(eyes)*　*hearing (ears)*　*smell (nose)*

Jobs for the brain

The brain sorts out the messages it receives from the nerves. Look at the picture on the left to see which parts of the brain sort out the messages related to your senses.

nerves—*special structures (like wires) that run from the brain to all parts of the body*

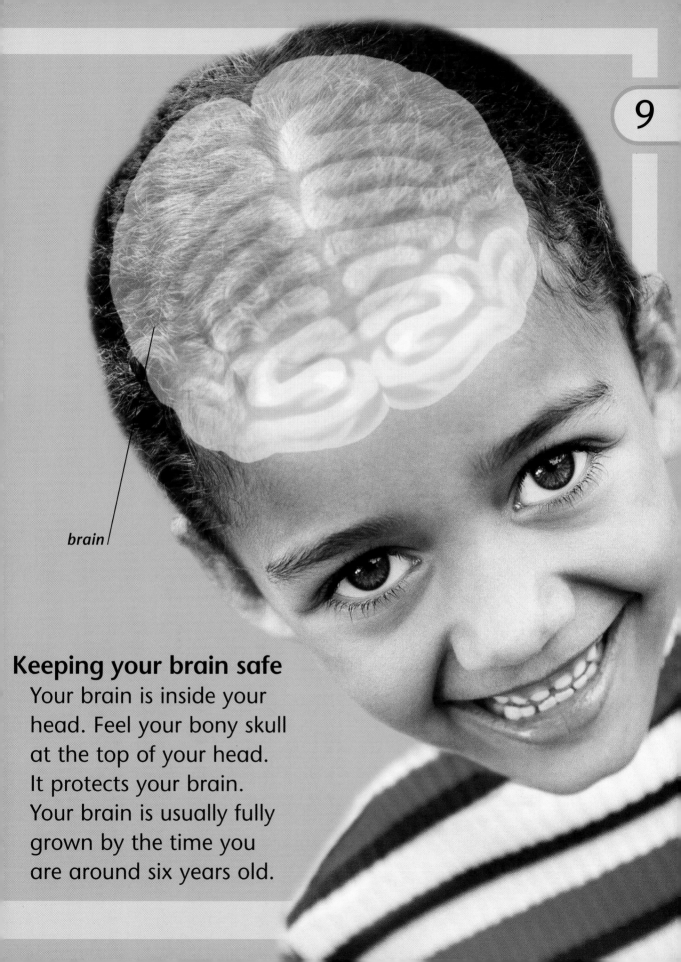

brain

Keeping your brain safe

Your brain is inside your
head. Feel your bony skull
at the top of your head.
It protects your brain.
Your brain is usually fully
grown by the time you
are around six years old.

How do I see?

Your eyes make pictures of the outside world—similar to what a camera does. You can see big things and small things, and you can see many different colors.

pupil (black)

iris (brown)

Letting in light

The black circle in the middle of your eye is called the pupil. This is an opening through which light passes into your eye.

Eye color

The colored part of your eye is called the iris. It can be blue, green, or brown. What color irises do these children have?

lens—*part of the eye that focuses light*

Making a picture

When you look at something, light bounces off of it and goes into your eye. Inside the eye the lens makes an image on the area called the retina, at the back of the eye. Messages about this image travel along nerves to the brain.

iris

retina

pupil

lens

nerve

bone in eye socket

Amazing eyesight

Some animals have excellent eyesight. Their eyes need to be right for the jobs they have to do—such as spotting food or watching out for danger.

Night eyes

Hunting animals, such as this cat, have powerful, forward-facing eyes that help them see details well and also judge exactly where something is. Cats can see much better at night than we can.

Sharp sight

Birds of prey, such as this peregrine falcon, can see things from a long distance away. Its large, alert eyes can spy a tiny mouse from high up in the air.

All-around view

Side-facing eyes help this mouse see as much of what is going on around it as possible. This means it can spot any enemies—and has a chance to escape!

prey—*an animal that is hunted and eaten by other animals*

Different eyes

Not all animals have eyes like ours. Some animals have eyes that look very different but are perfect for helping them find food.

Spider eyes

Most spiders have eight eyes. But only the two large eyes in the front are used for seeing. The smaller ones sense movement and help the main eyes find prey.

Two directions

The chameleon stays very still as it watches for insects to catch. Its big, bulgy eyes can swivel around and even point in two different directions at once.

Mini eyes

A dragonfly's eye is made up of 30,000 parts. Each one is like a tiny eye. These allow the dragonfly to see many images at high speed so that it can track fast-moving prey.

chameleon

***swivel**—to turn around in one spot*

How do I hear?

Your ears allow you to hear sounds, from a quiet whisper to the loudest music. The outside parts of your ears pick up sounds and funnel them down inside your ears.

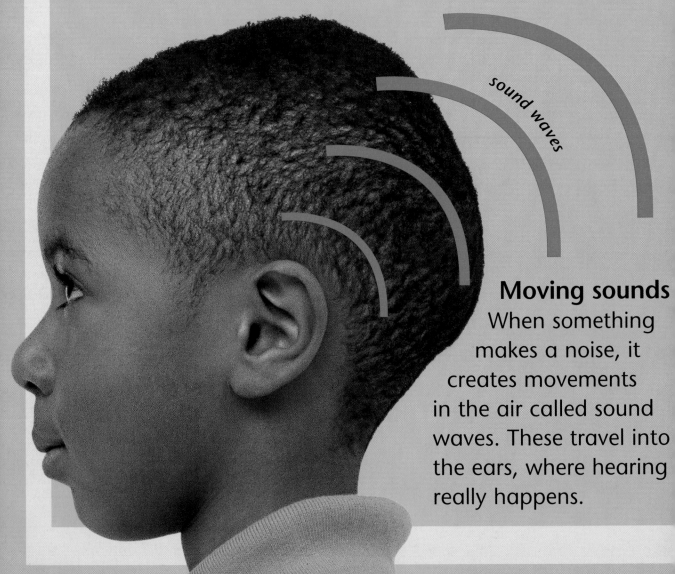

sound waves

Moving sounds
When something makes a noise, it creates movements in the air called sound waves. These travel into the ears, where hearing really happens.

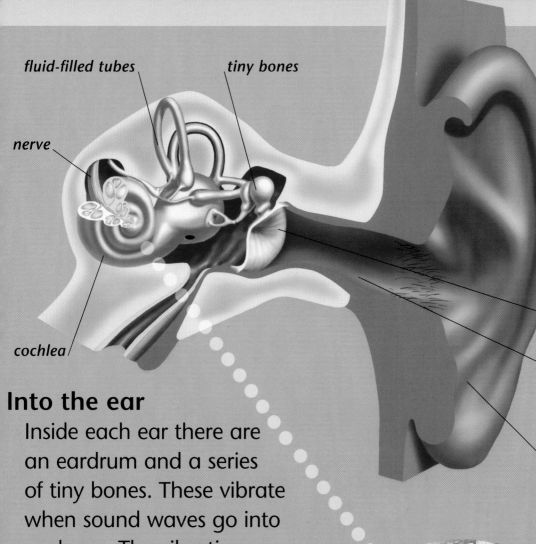

fluid-filled tubes

tiny bones

nerve

cochlea

eardrum

ear canal

outer ear

Into the ear

Inside each ear there are an eardrum and a series of tiny bones. These vibrate when sound waves go into each ear. The vibrations travel straight into the ears.

Tiny hairs

Deep inside the ear, in the cochlea, are more than 15,000 tiny hairs. When sound vibrations reach these hairs, they move and send nerve messages to the brain—and you can hear.

vibrate—*to move rapidly back and forth*

Staying balanced

As well as allowing you to hear sounds, your ears help you keep your balance. As you move around, tiny hairs in fluid-filled tubes inside your ears tell your brain if you are standing up or lying down.

Seasickness

You may feel sick on a boat because your brain gets confused. Your ears tell it that you are moving, but your eyes say that you are not.

Dizzy spells

If you spin around and
then suddenly stop, your
ears do not get the message
to your brain right away.
Then you feel dizzy.

Practice makes perfect

Gymnasts do not get dizzy
because they practice their
moves over and over again
so that their brains get
used to the signals.

Animal ears

Ears come in all shapes and sizes. The ears of the African elephant are the biggest of all. They can be more than six feet long.

Listening for danger

A rabbit's long ears help it catch the tiniest sound that could mean danger is close by. It can also swivel its ears to pick up sounds from different directions.

Faraway calls

Elephants can hear much deeper sounds than we can. They can hear the low calls of other elephants from several miles away.

Insect ears

Some insects have ears in surprising places. Crickets have ears on their front legs. This grasshopper has its ears on both sides of its body.

Listening underwater

The ocean may look like a silent world, but it is not. Sounds travel farther through water than air, and fish, whales, and other creatures can hear these sounds.

Closed ears

An otter does not use its ears underwater. When it dives, it closes its ears so that it will not get water in them.

Whale calls

The only parts of a whale's ears that you can see are tiny holes on each side of its head. But whales have excellent hearing. A humpback whale can hear the calls of other whales from many miles away.

humpback whale

Listening fish

Fish have ears inside their bodies that allow them to hear what is going on around them. They make noises to stay in touch with each other and to listen for the sounds of enemies—or food!

Sound pictures

Bats, whales, and dolphins are some of the creatures that have a special sense called echolocation. This means that they use sound instead of sight to make a "picture" of their surroundings.

Night hunters

Bats hunt at night and can catch an insect in complete darkness by using echolocation. As it flies, a bat makes many very high sounds . . .

echo—sound that bounces off of an object

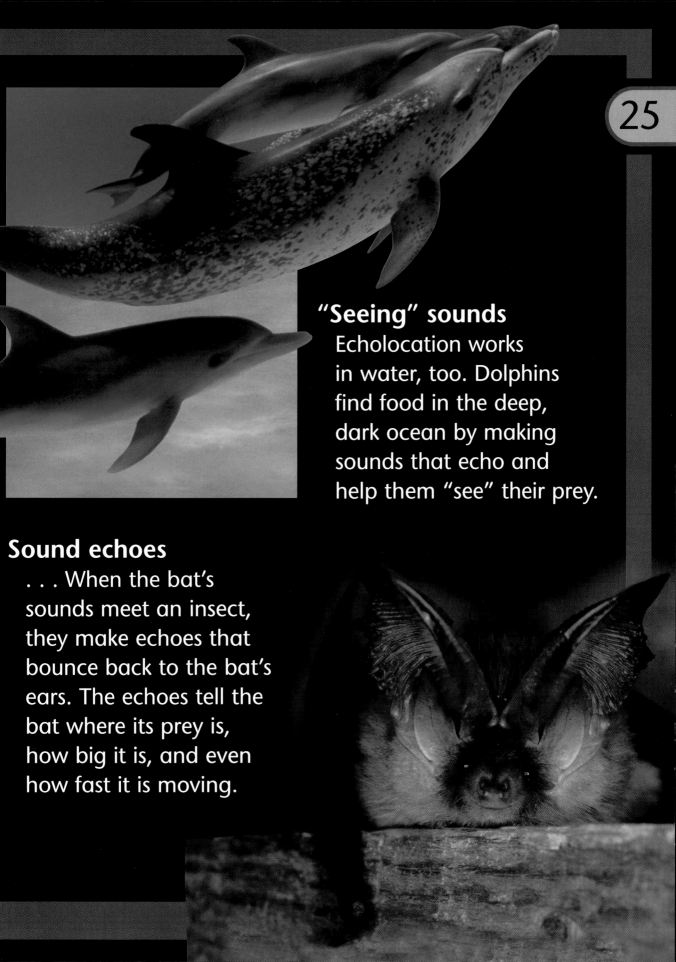

"Seeing" sounds

Echolocation works in water, too. Dolphins find food in the deep, dark ocean by making sounds that echo and help them "see" their prey.

Sound echoes

. . . When the bat's sounds meet an insect, they make echoes that bounce back to the bat's ears. The echoes tell the bat where its prey is, how big it is, and even how fast it is moving.

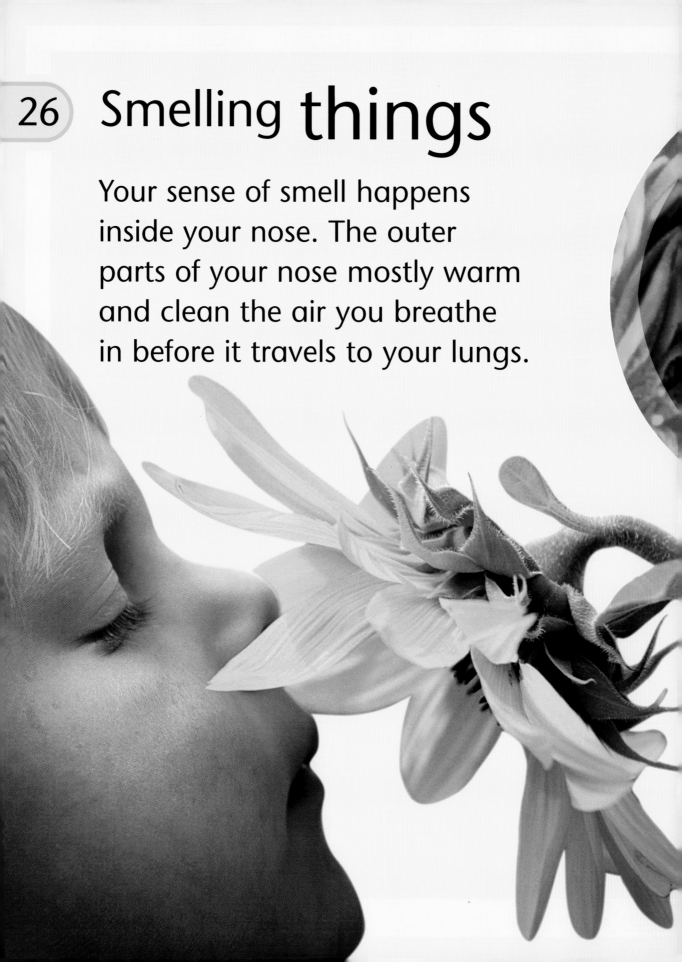

Smelling things

Your sense of smell happens inside your nose. The outer parts of your nose mostly warm and clean the air you breathe in before it travels to your lungs.

Achoo!

You sneeze when something irritates the inside of your nose and your body tries to force it out. The tiny hairs in your nose trap dust and dirt and stop it from getting into your lungs.

How you smell

When you smell something, tiny pieces of its scent travel into your nose. They go right to the top into two special sense areas. Nerves send messages from there to your brain, telling it about the smell.

lungs—two large, spongy bags in your chest that you use for breathing

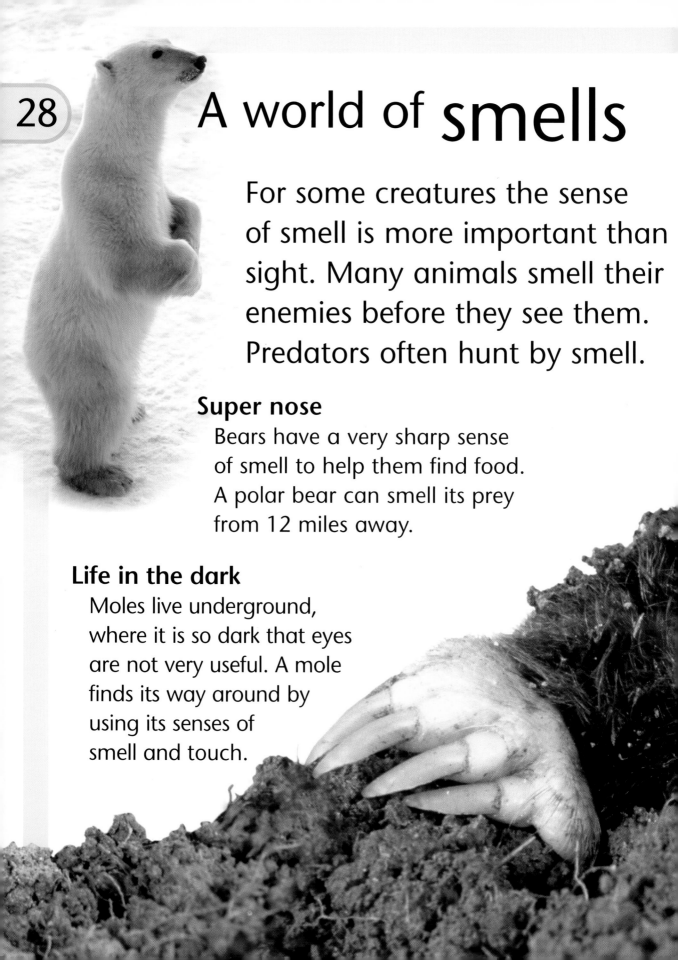

A world of smells

For some creatures the sense of smell is more important than sight. Many animals smell their enemies before they see them. Predators often hunt by smell.

Super nose

Bears have a very sharp sense of smell to help them find food. A polar bear can smell its prey from 12 miles away.

Life in the dark

Moles live underground, where it is so dark that eyes are not very useful. A mole finds its way around by using its senses of smell and touch.

Smell check

Every once in awhile
deer take a break from
feeding on grass and
look up to sniff the air
for any signs of danger.

Smelly messages

Many animals use smell to send messages to each other. These messages might say, "Stay away" or "I am looking for a mate." When a dog sniffs a tree, it can tell which other dogs have marked the same spot.

Special signals

When a female moth is ready to mate, she gives off a special scent. The feathery antennae on a male moth's head can pick up the smell from three miles away.

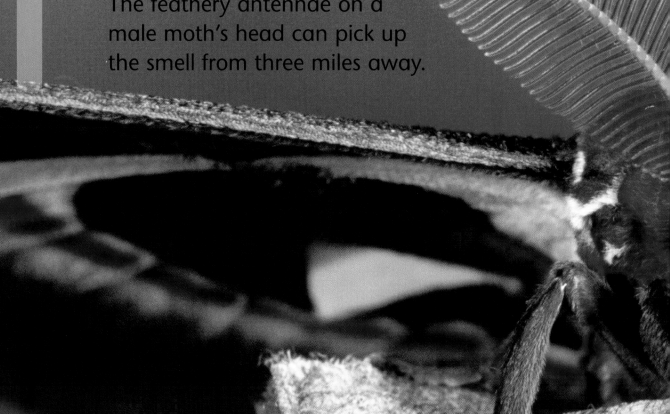

Smelly warning

A skunk uses smell to protect itself. If an enemy comes too close, a skunk squirts out a very smelly liquid from an area close to its tail.

My mark

When a cat rubs its cheeks against something, it is leaving a scent message. It is saying, "I was here. This is my patch."

Animal tastes

Like us, animals have taste buds on their tongues, but it is impossible to find out exactly what they can taste. Most animals probably use smell and taste to tell what is good to eat.

Good taste
Tigers—and pet cats—
have sensitive tongues.
They can taste
different flavors
in plain water.

Swimming tongues

Catfish are like swimming tongues—they have taste buds on their bodies that help them find food in the water. They can also taste food using their whiskers, which are called barbels.

Tasting toes

Butterflies taste with their feet as well as with their mouths. By using their feet, they know what type of food they have landed on before they unroll their tongues to eat.

Touch and feel

You can feel with every part of your body because your skin contains many tiny nerve endings. These send messages to the brain about what you are touching.

soft

cold

What does it feel like?

When you hold something, notice how it feels. It might be rough or smooth, sharp or soft, hot or cold. Our sense of touch tells us these things. It also lets us feel pain.

sharp

smooth

hot

Sensitive skin

Some parts of your
skin can feel things
better than other parts.
Fingers, toes, and lips
are very sensitive. Most
of your skin is covered
with tiny hairs. These
stand on end when you
are cold or scared—and
you get goose bumps.

Animal touch

Animals feel things with their skin, too. But some have extra ways of touching. Many animals have very sensitive whiskers that help them learn about their surroundings.

Super trunk

The tip of an elephant's trunk is the most sensitive part of its body. It does many things with its trunk, from stroking its young to picking up tiny leaves.

whiskers—*long hairs on an animal's face*

Hairy legs

A spider waits on its web for its prey. Hairs on the spider's legs sense the tiniest movement that could mean that food is close by.

Wet paws

A raccoon has very sensitive paws as well as whiskers. They are even more sensitive when they are wet, which might be why a raccoon wets its paws before eating.

Optical illusion

Which line is longer?
Seeing involves your brain as well as your eyes. Sometimes your brain can be tricked into seeing something that is not really there.

You will need
- Paper
- Colored pen or pencil
- Ruler

Using a ruler, draw a straight line that is 3 in. long. Draw another 3 in. line beside the first line, around 2 in. away.

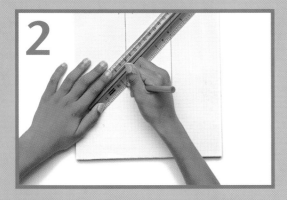

On the first line draw arrowheads pointing inward. On the second line draw arrowheads pointing outward, as shown in step 3.

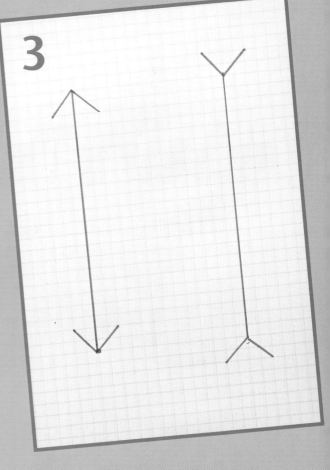

Look at the straight lines. Does one look longer than the other? The directions of the arrowheads trick your brain into thinking that one line is longer than the other.

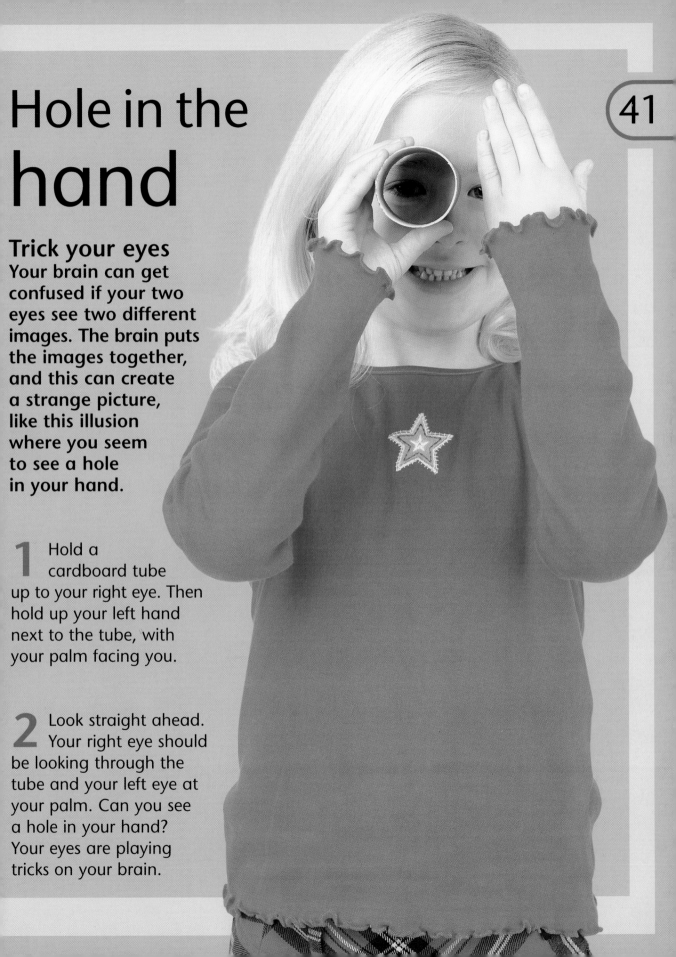

Hole in the hand

Trick your eyes

Your brain can get confused if your two eyes see two different images. The brain puts the images together, and this can create a strange picture, like this illusion where you seem to see a hole in your hand.

1 Hold a cardboard tube up to your right eye. Then hold up your left hand next to the tube, with your palm facing you.

2 Look straight ahead. Your right eye should be looking through the tube and your left eye at your palm. Can you see a hole in your hand? Your eyes are playing tricks on your brain.

Model eardrum

How hearing works

Make a loud noise, and you will see the stretched balloon on your model eardrum vibrate—just like your real eardrum does.

You will need
- Balloon
- Scissors
- Plastic cup
- Rubber band
- Rice grains

Use scissors to cut the end off of a balloon. Then carefully cut down along one side so that you can open the balloon out flat.

Cut the opened-out balloon in half so you have a piece big enough to fit over the top of your plastic cup. This will be the eardrum itself.

Stretch the balloon over the cup. Attach it using the rubber band, keeping the balloon stretched as tightly as possible.

Sprinkle some rice grains on top of the balloon. Clap your hands or shout. Watch the grains jump as the stretched balloon vibrates.

Listening game

Listening game

What can you hear?
Find a quiet spot and play this game—you will be surprised at the number of different sounds you hear.

You will need
- Notebook
- Pen

Sit down with your notebook and pen. Listen carefully for sounds—a noisy car, birds singing, or a dog barking. Write down or draw pictures of the things that you hear.

Taste and smell

Guess the smell

You will be surprised by how difficult it is to tell what things are without looking at them, using only your sense of smell.

You will need
- Scarf
- 5 plastic cups
- 5 smelly things: vinegar, a doughnut, chocolate, a banana, and toothpaste

Ask a friend to sit down and tie a scarf over his or her eyes. Make sure it is tight enough that he or she cannot see but not so tight that it hurts.

Add one smelly thing to each plastic cup. Then hold the first cup under your friend's nose and ask him or her to take a good sniff.

Ask your friend to smell and guess what is in the cup.

Give your friend the other foods to smell one by one. See how many he or she can guess correctly.

Guess the taste

Try guessing different drinks by taste alone. It can be difficult when you cannot see them, especially if some are similar.

You will need
- Scarf
- 5 plastic cups
- 5 drinks: milk, chocolate milk, orange juice, apple juice, and water

Just like in the smelling game, ask a friend to sit down and tie a scarf over his or her eyes. Make sure that he or she is comfortable but cannot see.

Pour five different drinks into the plastic cups. Make sure that you ask an adult which drinks you can use.

Ask your friend to take a sip of the first drink and guess what it is. Ask him or her to try each one and see how many he or she gets right.

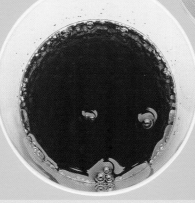

Make a touch cube

Test your touch

This is a fun way to test your sense of touch. When you have made the cube, you can play with it or play a touch guessing game.

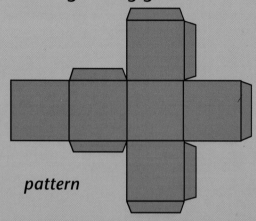

pattern

To make your touch cube you will need to cut out a piece of cardboard in the pattern shown above. You might need to ask an adult to help you copy it.

You will need

- Stiff cardboard
- Cardboard square
- Scissors
- Pen
- Ruler
- Glue
- 6 different textured items: we used velvet, corrugated cardboard, a cotton pad, tinfoil, sandpaper, and cereal shapes

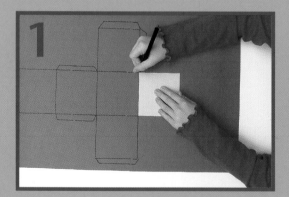

Place your cardboard square on the cardboard. Trace around it six times to make the pattern. Add flaps where shown in the pattern.

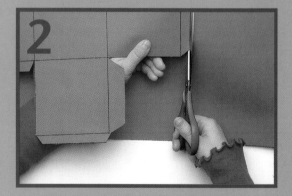

Carefully cut around the outside of the pattern, keeping all the edges as straight as you can. Then fold along all the lines.

3

Hold the middle square down with your finger and fold up the sides to make a box shape. Glue down the flaps to stick the box together.

4

Take some cereal shapes and carefully glue them onto one side of the box to make a rough texture. You can use any type you want.

5

Glue a different textured item onto each one of the other sides to make your cube. Ask a friend to guess the different items just by touching them.

Index